MW01617154

1 HOUR ANNUAL MARKETING PLAN

FOR PLASTIC SURGEONS AND MED SPAS

by

KELLY SMITH

© 2019

Copyright © 2019 Kelly Smith

All rights reserved. No part of this book may be reproduced, stored in a retrieval system or transmitted in any form or by any means without the prior written permission of the publisher.

Disclaimer

The material contained in this book is provided for educational and informational purposes only. The information provided is accurate and effective to the best of the author's knowledge. The author will not be held responsible for any outcome resulting from the use of this information.

This book is dedicated to Chloe, Kole & Karl, my loving family who are patient beyond measure! Thank you for allowing me the time to create business that I love, while making every effort to balance time and energy for you. My sister and parents have always been my biggest source of encouragement and strength and I am forever grateful to them for all the years of love and support.

"Working with Kelly and her team at PGC has been a truly positive experience for our Facial Plastic Surgery practice. PGC's team creates creative, eye catching campaigns that drive social media interactions as well as in office marketing materials. They have most certainly increased our social media presence while helping us transfer online interactions and referrals into paying, happy patients. Not only have they freed up our valuable staff from trying to manage our website, marketing and social media efforts, but they bring to the table a vast knowledge of industry market trends. They are a valued partner in our growing business."

Chad A. Glazer, MD - Glazer Facial Plastic & Cosmetic Surgery - Michigan City, IN

"I have benefited from Kelly and her team's extensive knowledge of the business side of operating an aesthetics business. PGC has vast experience with various technologies, they can give me unbiased advice on what they have seen work in other offices.

Additionally, I have worked with them for over a year running my social media for my office. It has been a great benefit to our growth and a weight off my team."

Brian Stolley, MD – President, MediSpa Maui - Maui, HI

"Our work with Kelly Smith and the PGC Team has included launch events, sales and marketing and an ongoing social media and digital marketing relationship for one year. Their ability to guide us through converting insurance pay patients to cash for service clients has been a vital part of our growth and success."

Scott T. Guenthner, MD - Plainfield, IL

"Excellent delivery of technology highlights. Helped secure multiple patient leads and procedures. Very friendly, approachable and professional. Overall excellent performance!"

Jordan P. Sand, MD - Spokane, WA

"We needed direction and planning help and it was 100% delivered! PGC helped with absolutely everything, she was attentive to all my requests and questions and did a wonderful job orchestrating the event with us. It was a major success! Thank you for helping us!"

Dr. Coville, Cornerstone Plastic Surgery and Aesthetic Medicine, New Jersey

I have purchased many lasers since opening my medical spa in 2003. The marketing & product support I have received from the PGC team has been exceptional and utterly unmatched by any other laser company or device company."

Dr. Amidon, LaserSpa@610, New York

"I really appreciated the YouTube videos you had on having launch events and social media. Thank you for your advice, it was very helpful. My consultant was very enthusiastic and had a log of great ideas and tips."

Lá-Shaun Elliott, MD - Hale Health Care - Woodstock, GA

TABLE OF CONTENTS

1. Why is it Crucial to Have an Annual Marketing Plan?   **1**
1.1 How an AMP Creates Revenue and Profit   1
1.2 Case study   1
1.3 Essential strategies   2

2. How to Build an AMP   **7**
2.1 AMP tool   7
2.2 AMP self-diagnostic assessment   9
2.3 Identify which services to cross-promote   10
2.4 Reaching your target market   11

3. Key Elements of an AMP   **15**
3.1 Creating cross-promotions and value-added offers   15
3.2 Social media integration and giveaway contests   18
3.3 E-mail marketing   21
3.4 Vlogs and blogs   21
3.5 Quarterly sales events   23

4. How to Build A Successful Promotion   **27**
4.1 Layer your messaging   27
4.2 Design a powerful graphic   27
4.3 Image selection   30
4.4 Sharing your promotional graphic   30

5. Putting It All Together   **33**
5.1 Planning checklist   33
5.2 Website maintenance   33
5.3 E-mailing for conversion   34
5.4 Blogging: What, when and how   34
5.5 Vlogging: What, when and how   37
5.6 Patient e-mailing with ROI   37

6. Social Media and Your AMP   **43**
  6.1 Social media self-diagnostic assessment   43
  6.2 Creating your graphics   43
  6.3 Content and strategy overview   45
  6.4 Building your editorial calendar   47
  6.5 Key terms in social media marketing   48
  6.6 Strategies for increasing organic reach   49
  6.7 Putting it all together   51
  6.8 Recommended tools   60
  6.9 Brand management on social media   61

7. Implementing an AMP in Your Practice   **69**
  7.1 Next steps   69

Resources   **73**

1

WHY IS IT CRUCIAL TO HAVE AN ANNUAL MARKETING PLAN?

1. WHY IS IT CRUCIAL TO HAVE AN ANNUAL MARKETING PLAN?

1.1 HOW AN AMP CREATES REVENUE AND PROFIT

Over the past decade, we have worked with thousands of physicians in the aesthetic industry. It is clear that the three key areas of strategy required for growth and profit are *finance*, *operations*, and *marketing*. Of all the systems and processes that will help your practice grow, the most impactful strategy is implementing an annual marketing plan (AMP).

Having a solid AMP in place will increase revenue, reduce impulsive marketing spending, direct patients to new services, maintain your bottom line, even out cash flow, and create high surges of revenue through quarterly sales events. Failing to create and implement an AMP is the most expensive mistake a practice can make, as it inevitably results in stagnation, confusion, and the need to discount services.

The four key essentials of an AMP are monthly cross-promotions, social media planning, e-mail marketing, and quarterly sales events. Implementing an AMP increases profitability and organization, and ultimately yields happy patients and repeat business.

By strategically narrowing your marketing focus and strengthening the cohesion of your overall message, you will reach new clients and increase your conversion and closing ratios.

1.2 CASE STUDY

We recently worked with a med spa in the Midwest that had been in business for seven years and whose marketing costs were impacting profitability. The challenge they faced was to grow without spending all of their profits on lead generation and marketing.

We recommended an AMP that included monthly social media contests, weekly e-mails to clients, and replaced their discounting strategy with cross-promotions. As a result, they saw a dramatic increase in sales of their most profitable service—a minimally invasive procedure. Within 13 months, they doubled their net profit *despite decreasing their marketing spend by 15 percent.* To date, they continue to implement an AMP consistently— resulting in loyal patients and consistent referrals.

1.3 ESSENTIAL STRATEGIES

Cross-promotions

Which services do you want to grow? Which areas are most profitable for you?

Your answers to these questions will help you to select the appropriate products and services that you'll use in your cross-promotions. Cross-promotions will be selected for each season and for your target clientele—primarily composed of women between the ages of 19 and 64.

We have the most success with value-added promotions that offer savings of 20 percent. Cross-promotions give clients what they want for free, as a reward for trying something new. It is an effective method of creating exposure for a product or service that might be difficult to sell on its own. Let's say your cross-promotion offers a free toxin with a laser series—you have your two talking points for the month. Toxins, series, and products are particularly suitable for cross-promotion because they are typically done quarterly.

Facebook/Instagram Giveaway Contests

Monthly Facebook and Instagram giveaway contests yield the best results in social media marketing. A contest provides the WIIFM (*What's in it for me?*) that engages followers so that they'll comment, like, and share your offers. Having provided social media management to our clients for years, we've seen this tactic alone create up to three times growth.

Comments and shares are direct recommendations from your followers to their friends and associates. After all, the primary goal of social media marketing is to create online referrals that turn into qualified leads.

E-mail Marketing

E-mail marketing works. Sending a weekly e-mail (also referred to as an e-blast) to your patients yields the highest response. You can use a variety of topics in your e-mail campaigns to educate and interest your patients.

Quarterly Sales Events

Another key element in your AMP is the quarterly sales event. Quarterly sales events have proven extremely effective for conversion. The event is not an open house; it is a consultation in the round.

Keep a narrow focus for each event: body, breasts, face, feminine health, body contouring, or injectables. Pre-qualifying attendees is the best way to ensure high conversion. Achieve this by consulting with them and making helpful suggestions.

You can incentivize attendance by awarding door prizes and a grand prize. Be sure to limit the event to 30 attendees. This will allow enough time for each interested patient to spend 15 minutes in private consultation with the physician.

For more information about planning sales events, please refer to my e-book *1 Hour Sales Event* or contact my team at projectedgrowthconsulting.com. We'll be more than happy to help!

2 HOW TO BUILD AN AMP

2. HOW TO BUILD AN AMP

2.1 AMP TOOL

> **What:** Create a marketing plan for the entire year in one hour. The key elements of the AMP are monthly cross-promotions, sales events, and social media content.

> **Why:** Your goal is to attract new clients and sell deeper to your existing client base. I'll explain what makes this unique in the aesthetic industry.

> **How:** Using a Gantt chart as your AMP tool, I'll teach you how to fill in your monthly marketing plan.

The Gantt chart in *Figure 1* (below) shows a sample AMP divided into monthly segments. For each month, we have highlighted the relevant focus area for cross-promotion, social media giveaway contest, blog and vlog topic, quarterly sales event, and website maintenance task. I'll walk you through preparing your own chart.

1 Hour Annual Marketing Plan

#	Sample Annual Marketing Plan	J F M A M J J A S O N D	Campaign	Offer or Date	Savings
1	Monthly Specials - This Mo Only		Post on website, FB, In office, E-blast each Tuesday	Limited to …people	Value of offer?
1.1	10 Years Younger This Year		Free Botox with Clear & Brilliant Series	5	$ 200.00
1.2	Lips and Lashes for Cupid		Free Latisse with any filler	5	$ 160.00
1.3	Shed your spots for spring		Free Microderm with IPL Series	10	$ 300.00
2	FaceBook Monthly Contest		Post 1st, award month end	Varied Prizes	Value of offer?
2.1	Botox		Free Botox 20 unites		$ 200.00
2.2	Filler		Free Latisse with any filler		$ 160.00
2.3	IPL		Free IPL		$ 300.00
3	2 Blogs/2 Vlogs Per Month		You Tube, Website, Blog, Social Media	Week 1 & 3	Week 2 & 4
3.1	10 Years Younger This Year		Free Botox with Clear & Brilliant Series	Toxin	Clear & Brilliant
3.2	Lips and Lashes for Cupid		Free Latisse with any filler	Latisse	Filler
3.3	Shed your spots for spring		Free Microderm with IPL Series	IPL	Microderm
4	Quarterly On Site Events		Concept and Prizes	RSVPs	Sales Goal
4.1	New Year New You		Body Event, 20% Savings, Grand Prize	30	Goal $50,000
4.2	Look 10 Years Younger		Injectable, Lasers, Retail, 20% off, Grand Prize	30	Goal $30,000
4.4	Exclusive VIP Event		Swag Bag, Discount Packages, Invite Only	30	Goal $40,000
5	Website Maintenance		On Going Website Tasks	Due Date	By Whom
5.1	Event Calendar		Update content, winners and blogs and photos	Quarterly	Office Manager
5.2	Monthly Specials		Post all in January for the year or quarterly	Quarterly	Office Manager
5.3	Gift Certificate Contests		Post first, award 31st. Select monthly amounts	Monthly	Office Manager

Figure 1. Annual Marketing Plan Tool

2.2 AMP SELF-DIAGNOSTIC ASSESSMENT

Examine your current marketing efforts by using the AMP Diagnostic Assessment found in the Resources chapter. Identify the areas where you'd like to improve performance. Next, take a few minutes to fill in the assessment to identify the strategies that may be missing from your current marketing plan.

You may find it useful to revisit these tools quarterly in order to benchmark your results.

1-877-742-0742
Info@ProjectedGrowthConsulting.Com
ProjectedGrowthConsulting.Com

MARKETING & SOCIAL MEDIA DIAGNOSTIC	YES =1/ NO =0
1 Do you run monthly specials?	
2 Do you utilize cross promotions instead of discounting?	
3 Do you host sales events instead of open houses?	
4 Do you have a client Email List?	
5 Do you update that list monthly?	
6 Do you email your clients weekly with different content and offers?	
7 Do you spend 5% of income on marketing efforts?	
8 Do you track the lead source in your system for all new clients?	
9 Do you know you average cost per lead?	
10 Do you run a report quarterly to look at which lead sources are the best?	
11 Do you look at your marketing budget by line item quarterly?	
12 Do you have an SEO program and or vendor?	
13 Are you consistently doing a PPC campaign?	
14 Do you utilize sales funnel methods to follow and drip on your leads?	
15 Do you automatically send out emails requesting patient reviews?	
16 Is your confirmation process automated by email or texting?	

Figure 2: Sample of the AMP Diagnostic Assessment

2.3 IDENTIFY WHICH SERVICES TO CROSS-PROMOTE

Which of the following are you trying to be? Circle 3 descriptors that apply to your practice.

Clinical atmosphere	Med spa atmosphere	Luxury atmosphere
Brand built on physician expertise and reputation	Emphasis on retail products	Emphasis on procedures
A few elective aesthetic services	Non-invasive to minimally invasive treatments (primarily facial & laser treatments)	Full range of treatments & services (cosmetic & plastic surgery)

✓ Where do you want to grow?

✓ Which are your favorite services to offer?

✓ What is your main challenge?

Which services do you really want to grow? Which areas are most profitable for you?

The answers to these questions will tell you which procedures, treatments, and products to utilize for cross-promotions. Remember to take seasonality into consideration when selecting monthly cross-promotions and scheduling quarterly events. This encourages a net profit-focused strategy for your AMP.

Cross promotions, events and contests improve customer service, show appreciation for your client base, and directly impacts profitability. In fact, it is between 5 to 25 times more expensive to acquire a new customer than it is to keep an existing one[1].

2.4 REACHING YOUR TARGET MARKET

In the aesthetic industry, your target clientele is predominantly composed of women between the ages of 19 and 64. Men typically constitute about 10 percent of a practice's patient base.

As you're designing your AMP, it's crucial to think about where and how you find your patients. Your lead sources are—in order of importance—online; patient referrals and staff referrals; and, your current patient base. I'll show you how to target each of these sources with every element of your marketing plan, so that you'll receive the maximum benefit.

Studies have shown that people need to see a message eight to ten times before they'll respond to it.[2] A decade ago, this would have been three to five times. The figure continues to grow as we are exposed to an increasing amount of input with each passing minute. Our phones are pinging us with e-mails, we hear commercials on the radio and see them on television, in print, and online. This is why you need to layer your messaging.

Different types of people respond to different forms of messaging. Some will watch a video blog embedded in an e-mail, some will look at your social media content, some will engage with in-office advertising such as flyers or video loops, and others might listen to your 'on-hold' voicemail greeting. In an upcoming chapter, I will explain how to layer your monthly marketing message, so that you're selling to people when they want to buy.

---

1   The Value of Keeping the Right Customers, Amy Gallo, Harvard Business Review.
2   *Rule of 7: How Social Media Crushes Old-School Marketing*, Kruse Control Inc.

PRO TIP

✓ We have established that the key strategies of your AMP are monthly cross-promotions, social media giveaway contests, e-mail marketing, vlogs and blogs, and quarterly sales events. Now I'll walk you through each of these elements and explain how to supercharge your efforts in every area.

3 KEY ELEMENTS OF AN AMP

3. KEY ELEMENTS OF AN AMP

3.1 CREATING CROSS-PROMOTIONS AND VALUE-ADDED OFFERS

We all know hard it is to resist the offer of a free gift with purchase. We want the free Lancôme bag with the lipsticks that aren't really our color, so we'll buy the eyeshadow palette and the mascara. Cross-promotion works exceptionally well in the aesthetic industry and provides you with two talking points each month. If you're offering free laser hair removal with body contouring, your message for the month can focus on both of these services.

Layer your monthly cross-promotion messaging by featuring it on your website, spreading it across all your social media platforms, highlighting it in your e-mail marketing, and displaying it on flyers in your office. This ensures that no matter how or where people hear from you, your message remains consistent.

With cross-promotion, the value add should amount to a discount of *at least 20 percent*. Offering less than this is unlikely to prove effective.

With surgery, consider using injectables as the added value. With new lasers, you can cross-promote with retail medical-grade products or ancillary services such as microneedling or microdermabrasion.

Cross-promotions will also increase customer retention. In fact, increasing customer retention rates by just 5 percent increases profits anywhere from 25 to 95 percent.[3]

---

3   *Prescription for Cutting Costs*, Bain & Company

In Chapter 4, I'll share detailed advice about designing your graphic. For now, here are the key elements that your graphic should contain:

1. Headline

2. Offer

3. Three or four main benefits or expected results

4. Offer value

5. Call to action (CTA): e.g. *click to book*, *call for a consultation* or *click here to accept this offer*.

When selecting which two of your services or products to cross-promote, consider the following factors:

1. Seasonality

2. Potential cost and profit

3. New treatments you'd like to introduce or services you'd like to promote

4. Your current clientele's favorite treatments or services

5. Vendor assistance with free products or treatments

ANNUAL · MONTHLY PROMOTIONAL PLANNER

MONTH	MONTHLY PROMOTION HEADER/TITLE	PROMOTION | VALUE	IMAGE #	APPROVED ARTWORK	WEBSITE	SOCIAL MEDIA	E-BLAST	SUCCESS OF PROMO (GREAT, OK, BAD)
Example	New Year, New You	FREE Botox with Laser Treatment - $250 Value	Face7	Yes | No	Date	Date	Dates	GREAT
JAN								
FEB								
MAR								
APR								
MAY								
JUN								
JUL								
AUG								
SEPT								
OCT								
NOV								
DEC								

Figure 3: AMP Promotional Planner

PRO TIP

✓ Why is cross-promotion preferable to discounting? Over the years, we've helped our clients sell millions of dollars' worth of aesthetic and med spa services, procedures and products. We've learned quite a bit about what it takes to win sales in this tough industry, and we've seen that cross-promotions are the key to selling more. While discounting can work for some practices, most practices can't afford to consistently offer them. Even though discounts of 50 percent are sure to bring in a few people, that doesn't help your net profit and many business failures are due to over discounting.

✓ Offering clients what they want for free as a reward for trying something new provides an effective method for bringing exposure to something that is difficult for you to sell on its own. Botox® and fillers are fantastic for cross-promotions. For example, you could cross-promote Botox® or Dysport® with microneedling, microdermabrasion or dermaplaning. In a cross-promotion, the service you offer for free should be something you know your clients love. This keeps your clients coming back every six to eight weeks.

3.2 SOCIAL MEDIA INTEGRATION AND GIVEAWAY CONTESTS

Results of a study published in the December 2018 issue of the Aesthetic Surgery Journal showed that patients base their choice of plastic surgeon more on their practice's Google rating and social media presence than on the surgeon's education and experience.[4] We have long suspected this, and this report confirms it based on unbiased research.

The article states, "Having a strong social media following is what now drives patients to plastic surgeons' offices." It continues, "Patients have increasingly been using online resources to make healthcare decisions and have a tendency to trust and value the rating that providers receive online."

Furthermore, below are some notable statistics from *The Ultimate List of Marketing Statistics for 2018*, posted on HubSpot.com.[5]

✓ 79 percent of people online use Facebook

✓ 76 percent of adults use Facebook daily

✓ As of June 2018, Facebook had 1.47 billion daily active users

---

4   *Aesthetic Surgery Journal*, December 2018.
5   *The Ultimate List of Marketing Statistics for 2018*, Hubspot.com

- ✓ Instagram hit 1 billion monthly users in June 2018

- ✓ As of January 2018, the age group with the most Instagram users is 18-24

- ✓ The age group with the second largest number of Instagram users is 25-34

- ✓ Americans open their phones over 150 times a day

- ✓ Americans spend hours per day on their mobile devices

There's no doubt that your clients are on social media. What impact does that have on your business? Digital marketing is everywhere your patients are. You cannot avoid digital marketing—it has replaced most traditional marketing methods.

You may be thinking, *Is social media really that important?* Let's look at some social media statistics before we get into the details of how content, consistency, and contests achieve your lowest cost per lead. We all know that patient, physician or staff referrals are the highest converting lead source. Social media is nothing more than a warm referral, friend to friend. The right social media will make your followers smile, fall in love with your practice and your staff, and feel like an insider!

Social media and video viewing are the two most popular online activities. In fact, Hubspot's list[6] notes the following significant statistics regarding video:

- ✓ 100 million hours of video content are watched daily on Facebook

- ✓ 64 percent of users are likely to buy a product online after watching a video

6   *The Ultimate List of Marketing Statistics for 2018*, Hubspot.com

Most business owners do not take the time to look at their cost per lead, ROI on social media or marketing by type. If you do, you will be leaps and bounds ahead of the competition and well on your way to creating a more profitable, steadily growing business. Most owners are in reaction mode, simply making it up as they go along. It's time to get results by implementing our strategies. You can create brand awareness, extend your reach and impressions, and inspire action by using social media to connect with clients. Engagement is key. In order to increase revenue using your social platforms, you must engage your followers.

Hands down, the best results we've achieved on social media were from monthly giveaway contests on Facebook. We've managed social media for many years for clients, and the giveaway contest is a surefire method for keeping followers engaged. Engaged followers will likely share your content, and that's when you'll experience exponential growth.

Outline your monthly contest for 12 months in your AMP. Periodically switching up the format of your giveaway contest provides variety and reinvigorates your loyal followers. For example, you can implement a surprise giveaway or run a "You Vote" contest and let your followers choose from three options. When applicable, we recommend that you connect the prize to the monthly cross-promotion. If you're offering a free series of chemical peels with a facial procedure, you might also offer a chemical peel as the giveaway prize for the month-long contest on Facebook and Instagram. Later in this book, I will go into more detail about how to run a social media contest.

Ask yourself the following questions:

1. Who in our practice is responsible for posting to social media?

2. Do we have the logins to all our social media platforms?

3. Do we have Facebook and Instagram profiles? Are these set up as business Pages?

4. Do we have a social media manager?

PRO TIP

✓ How do you engage people on social media? You create exciting and compelling posts with eye-catching and thought-provoking images. Posting to your social media should be an intentional task carried out as part of a clear strategy. Every post should serve a purpose.

3.3 E-MAIL MARKETING

It's time to embrace e-mail marketing. Send out a weekly e-blast to your patients. Studies show that e-mailing clients once a week yields the highest response.[7]

Share newsworthy items, such as events, flash sales, monthly promotions, and special offers. Vary the format so that you're not sending the same type of content each week. You can create different target lists by filtering according to gender, age, and type of procedure or treatment.

3.4 VLOGS AND BLOGS

Using your monthly cross-promotion as your starting point, integrate twice-monthly video blogs and written blogs in your AMP. If your monthly cross-promotion provides a free medical grade sunscreen with the purchase of an injectable filler, you might post a blog about your sunscreen offerings and another about fillers. If you've already blogged about these topics before, put a twist on it. For example, you could write about the differences between chemical and physical sunscreens. You could write about the anti-aging properties of hyaluronic acid.

7   *E-Mail Marketing Field Guide 2018*, Entrepreneur.com.

The blog posts can be used as outlines for video scripts. Enlist a staff member to record short video blogs using your mobile phone. A video blog should be a minute or less. Most viewers zone out after about 10 seconds. Nervous about video blogs? Dip your toe in the water by using an app like Boomerang from Instagram.

PRO TIP

- ✓ What are you going to promote this month—your Facebook giveaway contest or a quarterly sales event? Choose a single message and layer it across all of your communication, so that your patient will engage with your offer and respond to it.

- ✓ Whether through your video blog, Facebook Page or in-office advertising, layer this message consistently throughout all of your marketing efforts. Not only does this serve to improve Search Engine Optimization (SEO), increasing the likelihood that your website will rank higher in searches, but it helps you to reach your target clientele when and where they want to shop.

Planning Chart

	ANNUAL MARKETING PLAN						Promo Success
	Enter Your Monthly Promo Headline!	Promotion Value Added Cross Promotion	Limited To	Retail Value	Image Selection	Design Status	
EX:	New Year, New You! .....For example	Free Botox with any Laser Series	5	$300	SS #1258795	Final Proof	High, Med, Low
JAN							
FEB							
MAR							
APR							
MAY							
JUNE							
JULY							
AUG							
SEPT							
OCT							
NOV							
DEC							

Figure 4: AMP Gantt Chart Example

Action Items to Complete	Who	Date
Monthly cross-promotion: e-blast, post on Facebook & other platforms, update website		
Determine your monthly Facebook giveaway contest prize for the next 12 months		
Determine your monthly video blogs & written blogs for the next 12 months		

3.5 QUARTERLY SALES EVENTS

We suggest doing one event per quarter and outlining the basics for the events in your AMP as follows:

- ➢ Body-focused event: Spring

- ➢ Face or anti-aging event: Winter/Fall

- ➢ Feminine health event: Any time of the year

- ➢ VIP or holiday event with discounts on products and services: Summer/Fall/Winter

Customize your sales event schedule according to which treatments or procedures you offer. You might choose to alternate between surgical and non-surgical procedures. For example, your holiday event could highlight product and non-surgical discounts with live demonstrations of injectables and non-invasive body shaping. Perhaps your only elective medical procedure is for feminine health. If that's the case, you can hold quarterly events for that service only.

PRO TIP

✓ In the last year alone, we sold over $18 million in services for clients in our Onsite Sales Event Program.

✓ The keys to a successful event are narrowing your focus and pre-qualifying your event attendees. We've found that focused events generate the highest revenue. We also recommend taking an educational and consultative approach rather than a hard-sell approach.

✓ Schedule your event dates for the next 12 months and select a focus for each event. Choose dates that will allow you to secure the highest participation from your vendors and cooperation from your staff. Typically, evening events work best. If you throw in some appetizers and beverages, the mood at the event will be more intimate and relaxed. Perhaps one of your vendors will cover your catering tab or provide you with swag bag goodies, door prizes or a grand prize.

Action Items to Complete

Event Focus	Month	Date
Face Anti-Aging		
Body		
Feminine Health or Injectable		
VIP Client Appreciation Event		
Annual One Day Only Retail Sale		

4 HOW TO BUILD A SUCCESSFUL PROMOTION

4. HOW TO BUILD A SUCCESSFUL PROMOTION

4.1 LAYER YOUR MESSAGING

The two services you focus on in your cross-promotion should drive the whole marketing plan for that month. Consistency of messaging also serves to boost SEO.

Your goal is to get people to call you, to engage on your social media platforms, and to contact your practice using the form on your website—all of these constitute leads. Selling to your existing patient base and attracting new clients results in more people walking through your door, which ultimately increases revenue.

4.2 DESIGN A POWERFUL GRAPHIC

After you have selected your cross-promotions for the entire year—one per month for 12 months—it's time to create 12 promotional graphics to help you advertise.

BUILDING YOUR PROMOTION CHECKLIST

1	PROMOTION CREATION	
	What service are you selling?	
	What season or month is the target?	
	Who is the target demo?	
	What would they like for value added?	
	Create the headline	
2	IMAGE SELECTION	
	Select a seasonally appropriate image	
	Select an age appropriate image	
	Select a service appropriate image	
	Is the image attention getting?	
	Is the image what they aspire to be or your demo?	
	Is there direct eye contact?	
	Does this fit your website and marketing theme?	
	Is the image the right layout? Horizontal or vertical?	
	Does the image pull you emotionally into it?	
3	BUILDING YOUR PROMOTION	
	Offer of cross promotion is at least 10% value	
	Value is over $100	
	Less than 3 font types	
	3 Selling benefits	
	Fun and catchy headline	
	Just the details - you want them to call for more info	
	White space - make sure you have a lot	
	Review on a phone, that's where it is usually viewed	
	Keep it simple and eye catching	
4	URGENCY AND OFFER	
	While suppplies last or first 5 clients?	
	This month only or hard dates?	
	Call for details	
	Offer not valid with other promotions	
	No cash value	
	Non transferable	
5	PROOFING	
	Print out the promotion for proofing	
	Have multiple people proof	
	Check website, phone, address if applicable	
	Make sure the link goes to the correct web page	

Figure 5: AMP Promotional Builder Checklist Example

As you build a graphic for your cross-promotion, keep in mind that more than 70 percent of your web views will be on a mobile device, probably while the viewer is on the move and quickly scanning information. This means that you'll want to use very few words.

Your promotional graphic should have the following components:

Image: Select an image that supports the idea that you're trying to communicate. The image should be striking and have an impact; it should grab the viewer's attention and appeal to them on an emotional level.

Headline: Write a headline that hooks the reader and compels them to read further. Directly below, you should mention the *value added*—essentially the two procedures or services you are cross-promoting.

Selling benefits: Which 3 benefits does each procedure or service offer?

Call to action: The call to action compels the viewer to act on the offer by clicking the link or picking up the phone. It's best to appeal to their emotions, because we're selling a want, not a need. The following phrases emphasize urgency and exclusivity:

➢ While supplies last

➢ This month only

➢ First 5 patients

Look at the graphics below and consider how they achieve each of the elements we've just discussed.

4.3 IMAGE SELECTION

In this busy marketplace, a key part of the process is getting people's attention. Every practice will have its own style. It's essential to carefully consider what type of image will appeal to the demographic in your area. Some markets may lean more conservative (Lincoln, Nebraska, for example); other markets might be more liberal in their tastes and respond well to more flashy or edgy images (perhaps Miami, Florida). Choose your image wisely and keep your geographical area and seasonality in mind.

4.4 SHARING YOUR PROMOTIONAL GRAPHIC

After you have created your promotional graphic, be sure to save your document both in JPG and PDF formats.

Print version (PDF): The PDF is for printing. Make sure your printed flyer is scattered around the practice where people can see it. Display a large flyer in a pretty frame at the front desk, and position stacks of takeaway flyers in the waiting room, treatment rooms, and restrooms for patients to take home. This will inspire patients to initiate conversations with your staff and build awareness of your promotion and of the services you provide.

Online version (JPG): The JPG is for sharing online. Upload it to your website and share it on Facebook, Instagram, and any other social media platforms you're using, as well as in your e-mail marketing.

PRO TIP

✓ Visit www.shutterstock.com and www.stock.adobe.com for stock images.

Action Items to Complete	Who	Date
Research a few stock photo sites		
Create a stock photo site account		
Purchase a stock photo plan (i.e. Shutterstock)		
Start saving images for your promotional graphics		
Determine who will be responsible for creating the promotional graphics (in-house staff or outside marketer)		
Complete your first quarter of promotional graphics (3)		
Post on website, Facebook, Instagram		

5 PUTTING IT ALL TOGETHER

5. PUTTING IT ALL TOGETHER

5.1 PLANNING CHECKLIST

Now we'll break down the AMP checklist into quarterly, monthly, weekly and daily tasks that you can schedule in your calendar, and I'll share some tips about how to approach them.

- ➤ **Quarterly tasks**: Promote events, website updates

- ➤ **Monthly tasks**: Cross-promotion, Facebook giveaway contest, update social media cover art

- ➤ **Weekly tasks**: Posting 4 to 7 times, posting vlog, e-mail client list, post vlog on website

- ➤ **Daily tasks**: Respond to comments on social media

5.2 WEBSITE MAINTENANCE

Ask yourself the following questions:

1. Who on our staff is responsible for ensuring the practice website is up to date?

2. Do we have the URL, login, and password for our website?

3. Do we have a web admin to whom we can communicate changes?

4. Do we receive monthly analytics reports regarding our website's performance?

5.3 E-MAILING FOR CONVERSION

E-mail is a fantastic means of communicating with an audience who has signed up to receive information from your practice. They are interested in what you have to offer! In today's world of marketing, when a client gives a company their personal e-mail, it is a token of trust. That's why it is imperative that every e-mail blast you send out has value for them.

Content: Marketing e-mails do not always have to contain a promotional offer. E-mails are a great conduit for sharing links to your blog posts, announcing giveaways, and sending holiday greetings. When sharing content, always include a title, an image, a short excerpt of the text, and link to the original post on your blog.

Subject line: Your e-mail subject line is critical to the deliverability of your campaign. Studies have shown that 33 percent of people open an e-mail based on whether or not they like the subject line, and 69 percent of people will report an e-mail as spam based on subject line alone.[8]

5.4 BLOGGING: WHAT, WHEN AND HOW

A blog is a place to publish content related to your practice and specialties. Regular blogging helps to attract new potential clients and provides an opportunity for you to stand out as an expert in the aesthetics industry.

The most important rule to follow when developing your blogging content is to provide value. Be sure to address the questions that your existing and potential clients have about the aesthetics industry and your services. This way, you are being helpful and not pushy. If people who visit your blog are interested in your content and find value from it, they are more likely to come to you when they are ready to move forward with an aesthetic procedure.

---

8   *22 Eye-Opening Statistics About Sales Email Subject Lines That Affect Open Rates*, Hubspot.

Developing blog content isn't as difficult as it might seem. I'll share a few ideas to get you started. Your topics are the two services you are cross-promoting this month. Consider the following tips to create engaging titles and content for your blog posts.

> **FAQ blogs:** Keep a list of the questions your patients ask you about the procedures or services you are cross-promoting and answer each question with a blog post. Stick to the topic at hand, be honest, and provide as much insight as you can.

> **Number blogs:** Top 5 Results from Feminine Health Treatment; 3 Tips for Recovering Faster from Surgery; Top 10 Questions to Ask at Your Consultation.

> **Insider info blogs:** What do you think people really want to know about the industry? Describe a day in the life of your practice. Why is (insert service you're cross-promoting this month) the best solution for (insert problem)?

> **Keyword blogs:** Use SEO to your advantage by focusing your topic around popular search terms. Start by finding keywords related to the service you are highlighting this month.

Now that you have your content ideas, it's time to start writing!

Title: The key to writing a blog title is to think about how the reader would search for the topic online.

Title length: Keep in mind that Google will only show the first 50 to 60 characters of the title in the search results. We recommend using a free online character count tool such as charactercounttool.com to make sure your title is less than 60 characters. Another option to track your word count is by drafting your title in Microsoft Word.

Search-Engine Optimization (SEO): Optimizing content involves using keywords that will allow your content to be easily scanned by search engines. As a result, your content will come up higher in search results and reach more prospective clients. In a blog post, for example, the keywords should also be written into the body of the blog post in a natural, readable way.

Images: Don't overlook the importance of images. Images help to break up the content and keep the reader engaged. Stick to images that are relevant to the blog post. When uploading an image, you have the option of adding image-alt text. Always aim to add image-alt text, as this allows you to insert keywords and a description of the image to help search engines understand what the image is about.

White space, headlines, and bold font: White space or negative space is the portion of your blog post that contains no text or images. Leaving some space between paragraphs is very important for creating a visually appealing post. Headlines and bold font also help to break up a lengthy article and keep the reader engaged. Headlines are also a great way to highlight a keyword phrase.

Share buttons: Be sure to add social share buttons to your website so that readers can share your wonderful content with others. Your web developer should be able to help you to add share buttons.

Promoting special offers: At the end of each blog post, consider adding in an optional promotion. Offers in this section should be relevant to the topic of the post and should not be time sensitive. This can be a great way to convert the lead! Include a clear call to action (CTA), such as *Click here to book a complimentary consultation.*

VISIA or "what's possible" consult

5.5 VLOGGING: WHAT, WHEN AND HOW

With a vlog, you'll follow the same steps as above, but in video format. Vlogging and blogging really go hand in hand, and we recommend that for every topic you do both a vlog and a blog. Start by drafting your blog and use that to create the script for your vlog.

YouTube: For your vlog, upload the video directly to a video hosting service such as YouTube, and then embed the link in your blog post. When you upload to YouTube, make sure to include your keywords in the title and tag them in the video.

Social media: When sharing vlogs to your Facebook Page, we always recommend uploading separately to Facebook or Instagram instead of sharing the YouTube link. Uploading your videos directly to Facebook creates a dramatically wider organic reach.

PRO TIP

✓ Embed the video directly into your blog post for search-engine optimization.

5.6 PATIENT E-MAILING WITH ROI

Subject Line

What makes a good subject line varies according to the industry and the topic. Here are a few tips for developing an effective subject line in the aesthetic industry:

➢ **Pique the reader's curiosity.** Give them a brief idea about what's in the e-mail but keep it mysterious enough that they can't resist opening it to read the rest.

> **Add urgency, but only when the offer is time sensitive.** If you are trying to collect RSVPs for an upcoming event, feel free to infuse the subject line with a sense of urgency. However, it must really be time sensitive. If the e-mail is not time sensitive, the reader may feel that you've tricked them into opening it, and that can result in a higher unsubscribe rate.

> **Keep it short and sweet.** As most readers are viewing on their mobile devices, shorter subject lines are better. You wouldn't want them to miss the most important piece of the subject line.

Images: Pay attention to image sizes in e-mail campaigns. Most e-mail servers cannot handle a large image. It's best to keep images between 600 and 800 pixels wide.

Scheduling: Quite a few studies have been conducted about the optimal day and time to send e-blasts. At 10 a.m. on Tuesdays appears to be the best time to send marketing e-mails. Wednesdays or Thursdays would be your next best option. To get the best results, it's best to avoid Mondays and Fridays.

Studies suggest that 10 a.m. might be the perfect time to send an e-mail. Late morning e-mails generally receive the best open and click-through rates. Alternatively, you might schedule e-mail blasts for 8 p.m. through midnight, 2 p.m. or 6 a.m., as studies show that these are the times when people frequently check e-mail.[9]

Frequency: How often should you send marketing e-mails? This varies according to industry. In the aesthetics industry, we recommend weekly e-mails. Make sure your e-mails provide value to the reader and be sure to monitor your campaign results.

Tracking results: When reviewing campaign results, what trends are you seeing? Are people unsubscribing right away without

---

9   *E-Mail Marketing Field Guide 2018*, Entrepreneur.com.

even reading your campaigns? Do you have a high click-through rate? You should aim for a 2-3% click-through rate. By monitoring the results, you can learn to make data-driven decisions on content and frequency.

Hard bounce error: This means that delivery to the e-mail address has failed. A hard bounce can occur for a variety of reasons, but the bottom line is that if you receive a hard bounce you should remove that subscriber from your list. Many e-mail marketing software programs including MailChimp will automatically do this for you.

Soft bounce error: This means that an e-mail address is temporarily unavailable but can be kept on your list and tried again later. After several soft bounces, e-mail marketing software such as MailChimp will automatically remove the subscriber from your list.

Subscriber list: This is the list of clients' e-mails to whom you are sending your e-blasts. You can export this list from your Customer-relationship management (CRM) software (or wherever you're collecting client e-mails) and import it into your e-mail marketing account.

List segmenting: For experienced practices, we recommend segmenting your list into smaller targeted groups. Once you've added these segments into your e-mail marketing account, you can then send specifically targeted e-mails to the individual groups that would be most interested in that content.

Unsubscribed: This means that the reader of your e-mail has clicked the Unsubscribe link and wishes to no longer receive e-mails from you. A high unsubscribe rate can mean that your subscribers are not responding well to the content provided in the e-mails. This can also trigger an abuse complaint on your e-mail marketing account.

Open rate: The percentage of delivered e-mails that were opened by subscribers.

Click-through rate: The percentage of delivered e-mails that were opened by subscribers and received at least one click on any link within the e-mail.

Abuse complaint: You will usually see this message if more than one of your recipients mark your e-mail as spam. You should aim to keep abuse complaints to a minimum, as over time they can affect your sender rating. In extreme cases, an e-mail marketing company like MailChimp may shut down your account. If you're constantly receiving abuse complaints, try switching up your e-mail strategy with a softer call to action.

6 SOCIAL MEDIA AND YOUR AMP

6. SOCIAL MEDIA AND YOUR AMP

6.1 SOCIAL MEDIA SELF-DIAGNOSTIC ASSESSMENT

Your AMP elements are used throughout your social media strategy. We will now go through the foundation to create a successful social media process for your practice.

Take a few minutes to see where you are now and what might be useful to integrate into your social media strategy moving forward. Be sure to fill in the Social Media Self-Diagnostic Tool we've provided in the Resources chapter.

6.2 CREATING YOUR GRAPHICS

Now that you've developed your content strategy and structured your editorial calendar, we can move onto the fun part—creating the content. Even if you have a graphic designer, it is still important for you to have a basic understanding of design and available tools for times when you may need to create a graphic on your own.

Visualizing the Post

The first step is to consider what type of graphic and delivery will best showcase the content. For instance, if the content piece is a Before and After photo, would the message be better communicated via a single image, two images placed side by side, or in video format with the Before image dissolving into the After image? Visualizing the post prior to designing can streamline the process for each piece.

Graphic Sizes

In social media, there are several different graphic sizes for posts, profile images, cover photos, event cover photos, and advertisements. These can also differ according to platform, and they continue to change and evolve. If you'd like a current list of sizes for your graphic designer, we recommend bookmarking Sprout Social's guide (sproutsocial.com).

I'll show you some tools that remove the guesswork by providing templates based on graphic type.

File Types

Graphics come in many different file types. For social media, you will primarily be working with JPG images. The downside to JPG images is that they are non-editable and have a non-transparent background, and you cannot make them bigger without losing definition. For logos, you will want a JPG image, as well as a PNG with a transparent background for layering on top of the graphics that you design.

Stock Photo Resources

When designing your content, you will need stock photos to incorporate into your designs. Where do you find images to use in your designs? Can you grab them from Google search? *Absolutely not.* Photos that you find on Google are copyrighted content, meaning they are not free for you to use. There are, however, several free resources for stock photos that are safe for you to download and use in your social media designs.

Resources for free stock images:

Pixabay.com
Picjumbo.com
Unsplash.com

Gratisography.com

Paid resources (purchase by image or with a discounted subscription plan):

Shutterstock.com
Adobestock.com

Seasonality

Consider seasonality when you're choosing images to incorporate into your designs. Are you creating a February promotion for free Latisse®? Search for an image containing hearts. Is summer just around the corner? Find a great beach shot and overlay your text on the image.

Candid Photos

Don't underestimate the power of a candid shot from the office! These candid photos always seem to have a magical effect on boosting the engagement rate for a post because it allows the viewer to feel more connected with what makes your practice unique.

6.3 CONTENT AND STRATEGY OVERVIEW

Developing a great content strategy is crucial to running a successful social media presence for your practice. What is content strategy and why is it so important?

In a nutshell, content strategy is the strategic planning, developing, creating, and distributing of content. As straightforward as this may sound, many practices overlook the importance of creating a personalized content strategy. This can lead to confusion and ineffective marketing. An AMP is a useful tool to keep your plan on track because it breaks down promotions and giveaways by month. This results in a consistent message across your social media platforms.

Content strategy forms the foundation upon which you can build your social media presence. To build this foundation, you need to clearly define your purpose. In the aesthetic industry, your business is people, so your underlying purpose should be to develop connections, provide value, and educate about the aesthetic industry and services.

As you continue to focus on social media, you will identify goals such as increasing followers, increasing engagement, building a trusting relationship with followers, and converting them into clients by selling treatments or services.

- ✓ User-generated social media content has a 4.5 percent higher conversion rate

- ✓ 20 percent of people will read text, but 80 percent will watch a video

- ✓ People can recall 65 percent of visual content almost three days later

The above social media statistics[10] demonstrate that original content is the most engaging. Followers want to get to know you and your practice—this is why we encourage practices to share rather than sell.

Create helpful and entertaining content for your followers. Selling by technology name neither wins engagement nor widens reach. In order to get your followers excited about trying new treatments, you need to show them the *benefits* and the emotional satisfaction they'll gain. If you have the chance to share videos of puppies or babies or, even better, videos of puppies and babies, I highly recommend doing so.

---

10   *The Ultimate List of Marketing Statistics for 2018*, Hubspot.com

6.4 BUILDING YOUR EDITORIAL CALENDAR

The first step is to build your editorial calendar. The example below will help get you started. You can follow this example or use it as a guide for creating your own.

JANUARY

Sunday	Monday	Tuesday	Wednesday	Thursday	Friday	Saturday
	1 SERVICE BLOG GIVEAWAY WINNER POST	**2** FB AD: NEW LIKES	**3** FAQ POST	**4** AESTHETIC FUNNY	**5** GIVEAWAY POST	**6**
7 MONTHLY PROMO	**8**	**9** BEAUTY QUOTE	**10** SERVICE BLOG	**11** GIVEAWAY POST	**12**	**13** FAQ POST
14 VLOG: Q&A W/DR	**15** HOLIDAY: MLK DAY	**16**	**17** FAQ POST	**18** SERVICE BLOG	**19** GIVEAWAY POST	**20** AESTHETIC FUNNY
21	**22** SERVICE BLOG	**23** FAQ POST	**24** GIVEAWAY POST	**25**	**26** BEAUTY QUOTE	**27** MONTHLY PROMO
28	**29** GIVEAWAY POST	**30** SERVICE BLOG	**31** FAQ POST			

Remember that your content strategy is to develop connections, provide value, and educate people about the aesthetic industry and your services, treatments, procedures and products. Your goals should include:

1. Increasing followers on Facebook and Instagram.

2. Building a trusting relationship with followers by educating them, so that when they are ready to purchase, they will come to us.

3. Converting followers to clients by promoting services, treatments and special offers.

How you create your editorial calendar is completely up to you. Some choose to have a printable hard copy. At PGC, we prefer to use a shared digital calendar. A great option for a digital editorial calendar is Google Calendar.

When drafting your editorial calendar, you should plan to maintain a consistent posting schedule. Our years of experience in the aesthetic industry have shown us that the optimal frequency for Facebook and Instagram posts is between four and seven posts a week.

Later on, I will explain how to analyze your insights and make data-driven decisions to determine if you need to adjust the number of posts you make each week. But first I'd like to walk you through a few key terms.

6.5 KEY TERMS IN SOCIAL MEDIA MARKETING

Facebook algorithm: Each day, people, brands, organizations and businesses post a tremendous amount of content to Facebook. It would be impossible for any individual to keep up with all of it, so Facebook developed an algorithm to calculate which content should appear in each user's newsfeed.

More than 100,000 highly personalized factors are contained within it, and it is constantly changing. While Facebook keeps secret the exact equations of its ever-evolving algorithm, it has released bits and pieces of information that we can use in your content strategy.

Reach: Reach is the quantity of people who have seen your post or advertisement. When you make a post to your business Page, Facebook will deliver that post in the newsfeeds of people who have liked your Page and have chosen to follow you. It is important to note that Facebook will deliver your posts only to a percentage of your followers. This percentage varies according to a variety of factors, including the Facebook algorithm and advertising dollars.

Boost: The option to pay for your post to reach more people. If you choose to boost a post, we recommend doing so in small increments ($10, $20, $30) and using targeting measures to focus delivery.

Organic reach: Organic reach describes the number of people to whom your post was delivered without boosting (paying for the post to reach more people). You can increase your organic reach rate by strategically choosing your content. Later in this book I will provide some methods PGC has used to improve organic reach.

Engagement: Engagement in social media can be defined as interest, which is measurable in the form of likes, reactions, comments and shares by viewers of your content. As engagement is a significant factor within the Facebook algorithm, maintaining a high engagement rate by posting quality content will improve your Page's overall organic reach.

6.6 STRATEGIES FOR INCREASING ORGANIC REACH

Certain post types are more likely to gain high levels of engagement and interaction on social media. When a Facebook or Instagram follower comments, favorites or shares your post, they're announcing to the world that this post means something to them. You can picture it as a fishing net, and each time we cast that net wider, we're able to pull in more fish.

When your followers love your content and engage and interact with it, they're helping you to cast that net even wider. Your goal is to make your followers think *this speaks to me*. You must find what moves your audience and motivates them to engage positively with you, thereby increasing your organic reach.

How do you create posts that engage your audience? Take the time to ensure that every post has a purpose. People often ask us: *Should all my posts be about our procedures, treatments and products?* The answer is a resounding *No!*

If you're constantly selling products and services, your audience will tune out. Share varied and highly engaging content that expresses the personality of your brand, and your audience will connect with you and keep coming back for more. This is how you build brand loyalty and nurture relationships that develop into patients when they're ready to buy.

PRO TIPS

- ✓ Try following your monthly theme for the seasonal timeframe.

- ✓ Images are responsible for 75 to 90 percent of an ad's performance on Facebook. A recent study ran A/B testing using the same message with different images, and they performed very differently. [11]

- ✓ When crafting the imagery for your content, take your time and be creative. Keep in mind who your target clients are and think about what will resonate with them.

- ✓ It would be shortsighted to simply appoint a millennial staff member to manage your social media, because the skills involved in managing a business profile are vastly different from managing a personal profile.

---

11   *100K Facebook Ads Tested! Here's What Works*, Consumer Acquisition.com

6.7 PUTTING IT ALL TOGETHER

You should aim to include different types of posts in your editorial calendar. I'll walk you through the various posts and share advice about how best to utilize each one.

1. Technology/benefit post

You want your audience to know what you provide, so some of your posts should highlight your procedures, treatments and products—especially those you're featuring in your monthly cross-promotions. In addition to naming the technology, you must highlight results and benefits.

> **Here's how you might position laser hair removal:** *Brrr! Might be a little chilly now, but swimsuit season is just around the corner, so why not ditch that razor and give us a call? Let's talk about [insert technology name here]— the leading technology in laser hair removal! [insert your phone number] #lhr #hairfree #laserhairremoval*

> **Here is an example post for body contouring:** *Smooth curves ahead with body contouring & cellulite treatment. Confidence is sexy, so turn the volume up on your self-esteem. Consultations are free—we're ready to book yours today! [insert your phone number] #bodycontouring #cellulitetreatment #dimples #smoothskin*

2. Question post

To encourage your followers to comment on your posts, ask them a question:

> **New Year's**: Are you *for* or *against* making New Year's resolutions?

- **Valentine's Day**: Do you prefer roses or tulips? What is your favorite flower? Do you like chocolates or valentine hearts?

- **Mother's Day**: Would you rather have a spa day or go to brunch?

- **Thanksgiving**: Do you prefer pumpkin pie or apple pie?

- **Halloween**: What's your favorite kind of candy?

- **Cinco de Mayo**: Salsa or guacamole?

- **Fourth of July**: Sparklers or firecrackers?

- **Christmas**: Do you prefer a real Christmas tree or a fake Christmas tree?

- **Winter**: Hot chocolate or hot apple cider?

- **Spring**: What's your ultimate spring break vacation?

- **Summer**: One piece or two?

- **Fall**: What's your favorite thing about fall?

- **Winter**: Tropical or snow vacation?

People are eager to share their opinions, especially if the timing is perfect. If you can think of questions your followers will feel compelled to answer, you'll see your reach and engagement grow.

3. Testimonial post

Testimonial posts provide social proof by building trust and creating a positive impression on potential customers. People trust their peers, so this patient-generated content is valuable.

Draw on your Google reviews or patient feedback in post-op paperwork, on your website, or in e-mails or greeting cards. For example, you can turn your Facebook reviews into a post and make it visually appealing by including an interesting JPG image. With the patient's permission, you might take a photo of them with the physician or record a quick testimonial video (10 seconds will suffice). If a patient brings you thank you flowers or a sweet treat, take a photo of their gift and create a highly personalized post or a Boomerang.

4. Staff highlight post

Considering that personalized content makes successful posts, be sure to highlight your staff on social media. Your audience will love to see their favorite front-desk staffer who always greets them with a big smile, the nurse-injector who keeps their forehead wrinkle-free or the beloved physician that made their breasts look 10 years younger.

Highlight a staff member each week over the course of a month. To make this fun and interactive, you might start things off by posting a Throwback Thursday photo of a team member and revealing their name the following week. Highlight your team members' birthdays, special accomplishments, pets, babies, travel or staff events.

5. Before and After post

Before and After photos tell a whole story in an instant. That's why they are one of the most popular types of posts and why, according to patient surveys, are the most popular pages on elective medical websites. Have fun with your monthly theme and try to include Before and After photos for one of the two services in the cross-promotion of the month. Be sure to clearly label the photos and make sure that the After photo is clearly distinguishable from the Before photo. If the results pictured are dramatic, entice your followers to engage with your post by captioning the photo *"Can you guess the procedure?"*

6. Facebook/Instagram giveaway contest

Running a giveaway contest on Facebook and Instagram is an excellent strategy to increase your reach and engagement. You can incorporate a monthly giveaway to anchor your fans and keep them coming back for more, in addition to generating increased visibility before your quarterly sales event.

Step 1: Decide the goal of the contest

Your goal is to increase the visibility of your post and to spread awareness of your practice and the services it provides. You're aiming to maximize *reach* (the number of eyes that will see your post) and *engagement* (the number of comments and shares that your post generates).

You'll use the giveaway contest format to build awareness and keep your Page visible in the newsfeeds of your fans. Did you know that only one to 5 percent of your page's fans will see your posts in their newsfeed? Your goal is to increase that percentage. Holding a giveaway contest is one way to achieve that.

Now that we've established what *your* goal should be when running a contest, it's important to acknowledge that your *followers'* goal is to win.

Consider these contest ideas:

Service/procedure/product of the month: (For example, *Win Free Botox® this Month!*) This is a giveaway of one of the two items in your monthly cross-promotions. Be sure to highlight the benefits of the product or service, and that the photo shows the results and emotions that appeal to your target demographic.

You Vote: Invite your followers to choose the prize for this month's contest. For this strategy, the post would say something like: *Would you like the prize this month to be toxin, filler or laser?* Then they vote for their choice by commenting on your post. This is a win for you, because comments significantly expand your reach.

Mystery prize: This is one of the most popular. The prize is revealed when the winner is announced. Nobody knows what it will be until the winner finds out! Building suspense creates follower engagement.

Selfie or GIF giveaway contest for Facebook and Instagram: Invite your followers to post a selfie or a GIF (animated image file otherwise known as a 'little video clip') in the comments section. This will enter them into the contest.

'Win One | Give One' giveaway contest for Facebook and Instagram. This is a wonderful way to get new followers through friends by asking them to follow your Page. Try a 'Win One | Give One' contest where the winner will win two prizes, one for themselves and one for a friend. To enter, they should tell you in a comment to whom they would give the other prize. This type of contest is particularly popular when you run it in November or December, as it lines up well with the seasonal theme of giving.

Step 2: Determine the contest prize (a.k.a. the WIIFM)

WIIFM stands for *What's in it for me?* This is the question that your fans are asking themselves. What exactly will they gain by being engaged with your Page? This is a question of *quid pro quo*—they want something in exchange for their involvement. Ask your vendors to supply you with the prize.

Perhaps you have an extra syringe of filler or a sample vial of 50 units of Botox® from your Allergan sale representative.

Possibly you have some free SkinMedica® products you could put together as a skin care bundle. Trying to keep your aesthetician busy? Consider a free micro needling treatment, or a facial. If CoolSculpting® is a new offering at your practice, treat the winner to a CoolSculpting® treatment and use their photos to start building your Before and After photo collection. Be resourceful and creative to get the most mileage out of your dollars.

Step 3: Define contest rules and create a giveaway post

1. Pick an image that will speak to your fans. It should grab and their attention.

2. Add text to your image. For example: *Giveaway Contest* or *Choose your Prize Giveaway. Like, comment or share in order to enter to win the prize!*

3. Specify the end date of the contest (for example, at the end of the month).

4. Specify how and when the winner will be notified (for example, via Facebook in the first week of the following month).

5. Your contest must be legal. You are required to provide official rules.

6. The contest rules should be included in the post. Be sure to post them *underneath* the hashtags, so as not to distract from the giveaway post.

7. Make sure text is clear and keep word count to a minimum, since most users will be viewing this on a mobile device.

8. Post the contest on the first day of the month. Draw a name and announce the winner on the last day of the month.

Rules for running a contest on Facebook

➢ Only Business Pages can be used to run a contest. Do *not* run a contest from your personal profile.

➢ Make it clear that the contest is run by you, not by Facebook. You *must* include in your post wording to the effect that this promotion is in no way sponsored, endorsed or administered by, or associated with, Facebook.

➢ *Don't ask for a share*. No matter how you word it, this is a breach of the rules.

➢ *Don't ask for a tag*. Tagging is not a permissible entry requirement.

➢ Be sure to review the current Facebook Pages rules for promotions.

Rules for running a contest on Instagram

If you use Instagram to communicate or administer a promotion (such as a contest or sweepstakes) you are responsible for the lawful operation of that promotion, including the following:

➢ Staying informed on the official rules. These change often, so ensure that you stay up-to-date.

➢ Offer terms and eligibility requirements (e.g. age and residency restrictions).

➤ Compliance with applicable rules and regulations governing the promotion and all prizes offered (e.g. registration and obtaining necessary regulatory approvals).

➤ You must not inaccurately tag content or encourage users to inaccurately tag content. Don't encourage people to tag themselves in photos if they aren't in the photo.

➤ Promotions on Instagram *must include* a complete release of Instagram by each entrant or participant; and an acknowledgement that the promotion is in no way sponsored, endorsed or administered by, or associated with, Instagram.

Step 4: Choose the contest winner

If you run your giveaway contest for one month, posting once per week for four weeks, you can choose your winner from the fans who have commented on and/or tagged your four giveaway posts. There are different options for choosing a winner: choosing your winner manually or selecting one at random by using a tool.

Use a picker tool: There are several free tools available online to randomly choose the winner for you (i.e. Pick a Winner by Woobox). By using this method, you're able to stand tall if a fan cries 'Foul!' on your winner selection. When you use this method, you aren't taking into consideration any other criteria, such as the winner's location, age and gender. Some tools will allow you to set some parameters.

Maximize reach: You might consider picking the fan with the largest following as your winner. If their security settings are low enough that you can see the number of friends they have on their profile, then you know the probability of a high post reach is good. In turn, you have the ability for the winner's friends to now be aware of your practice and your Page.

Reward a loyal client: We all have those clients that we just love to see walk through the door—our handful of favorites. Particularly if they're an active presence on your Page, consider rewarding them for their loyalty. Chances are they'll post a wonderful comment after they win, and you'll be able to reach their friends with your post.

Engage with a very active fan: Let's say you have a fan who is active on your Page, but they've never been into the practice. Take a moment to snoop on their profile and see if they appear to be someone that could potentially be a patient. Here's your chance to attract someone new to the practice.

Step 5: Post the winner

It's time to post the winner! Create a fun graphic to announce the winner. You will not be able to tag the winner (@username) unless they comment on the post. In that case you can direct message the winner about winning your contest. This post will get a good reach and response.

Step 6: Contact the winner

We recommend that you look back at your giveaway posts and find the comment that the winner posted. Reply to their comment by saying, *Don't forget to check out our winner post today!* That will prompt them to look for the post and comment there.

Be sure to notify your front desk staff, so that everything will run smoothly when the winner calls in to schedule their appointment. Of course, if they're a current patient you will have their mobile number or an e-mail address; regardless, we suggest making an announcement post to inform everyone else who participated that the contest has ended, and a winner has officially been awarded.

PRO TIPS

✓ Consider asking your winner to pose for a photo with a staff member to post on social media to highlight your giveaway contest. Perhaps the winner will allow you to shoot a Boomerang or a short video of their treatment to use as well—it doesn't hurt to ask. If they want to maintain complete confidentiality, you can ask for a testimonial. Quote their feedback in a post and attach a stock image or an image you create.

✓ If you really want to increase your reach and engagement and potentially draw new fans to your Page, respond to *all* of the comments from your fans on your giveaway contest posts!

6.8 RECOMMENDED TOOLS

1. **Social media scheduling tools** will make your day-to-day posting easier, especially if you're going to be on multiple social media platforms. You can use Social Report, Hootsuite or Sprout Social to take one post with a graphic or a video and schedule it across Facebook, Instagram, Twitter and LinkedIn at the same time. These tools also come with reporting capabilities, so you can track your analytics to see how your social media is performing. Some also contain libraries of free images and GIFs, and a dashboard so you can comment back on all your post activity from one place.

2. **Spark Post** and **Canva** are two great apps for designing your posts. Without an in-house graphic designer, the task of creating promo and giveaway graphics can be daunting, but not with these apps! Both include a built-in free stock image library, and preset image sizes for various social media platforms and image types.

3. **Giphy:** A GIF is an animated image file. GIFs are a great way to add a little more excitement and movement to your posts. Much like videos, they're more interactive and entertaining than photos alone. We like using the GIPHY app to search for ready-to-use GIFs to include in our posts. For example, we might search for a congratulations GIF to use in a giveaway winner announcement post. Another way to put GIFs to use would be to ask Facebook fans to comment on a post with a GIF. For example: *Comment below with a GIF of your favorite movie!*

4. **Boomerang:** Another fantastic app for creating engaging animated posts. This is something you would use in office and is a supporting app for Instagram. Boomerang snaps a series of photos and edits them together in a mini-animated video. A great way to use Boomerang would be to have a new employee waving or an employee doing a happy dance for Friday. If you have a physical object to give away, use Boomerang to announce the contest by moving the product up and down.

6.9 BRAND MANAGEMENT ON SOCIAL MEDIA

Let's start with a recap of the most important social media strategies that have proven successful in the aesthetic industry.

Editorial calendar: Regardless of which form it takes, an editorial calendar provides a way to visually lay out your content so that you can plan, develop and schedule your content. Keeping an editorial calendar is *essential* to an effective content strategy.

Increasing organic reach: You can increase your organic reach by finding what moves your collective audience and motivates them to engage positively with you. Intentionality is key—every post must have a purpose.

WIIFM: *What's in it for me?* This is the question that your fans are asking themselves. What will they gain by being engaged with your Page? For their involvement, they want something in return.

Giveaway contest: Running a giveaway contest on Facebook is an excellent strategy to increase your Page's fan reach and engagement. You can incorporate a monthly giveaway to anchor your fans and their loyalty to your Page and keep them coming back for more. You can also use a contest to generate increased visibility on your Page as a lead-up to an event you're hosting.

Maximizing a giveaway: If you really want to increase reach and engagement, as well as draw new fans to your Page, be sure to respond back to *all* the comments from your fans on giveaway posts!

E-mail marketing: In today's world, giving a company your personal e-mail is a token of trust. That's why it's imperative that the e-mail campaigns you send your clients provide value to the reader. Having a clear focus for each marketing e-mail will help to ensure that you consistently deliver valuable content to your clients.

Importance of video: If you have a video embedded on your website, you are 53[12] times more likely to show up on the first page of Google! Video is an integral element of social media, so if it's not yet a part of your content strategy, now is the time to make it so.

Analytics: Use your Facebook Insights to check the demographics of your audience, and that will help you get an idea of what type of content your followers may respond to. As you publish posts daily, track the *reach* and *engagement* on each post to measure the success. A collective personality will start to form, and you'll be able to determine which post types really speak to your followers.

---

12   *4 Great Reasons You Should Use Video Marketing,* Moovly.com

Responding on Facebook & Instagram

Now that you've implemented your AMP, your Facebook Page and Instagram profile are starting to pick up steam. You're publishing some highly engaging posts and fans are leaving comments—mostly positive ones, with a few negative ones here and there.

What do you do now, besides giving yourself a pat on the back? Your next steps should be to respond and continue to build the momentum with your followers.

Set yourself a goal and appoint a staff member to reply to all comments, up to a reasonable limit. Engaging with fans strengthens your relationship with them, and it keeps them coming back for more. We want them to stay engaged with us so that when they're ready to purchase, we'll be at the forefront of their minds. The Facebook algorithm rewards posts with high engagement, which means you will remain more visible and be seen more frequently by your fans.

It's just like maintaining a relationship with a friend. If a friend is always reaching out to you and you never reciprocate, your friendship with them will suffer and may even fade away. Unanswered questions and comments can deter potential fans. With both Facebook and Instagram, be sure to turn on push notifications, so you will be notified when fans and followers leave comments and shares.

Social Media Marketing for Conversion

One of the ways we help our clients is by providing social media management. We started by helping a handful of clients with social media for their events. Over time, an increasing number of clients requested us to manage their social media for them. After five years of providing this valuable service, our waiting list is full of practices needing our help.

Our clients' social media follower growth averages 200 percent per year. That is an impressive number against the industry averages of Facebook Business Pages growing only 6 to 18 percent per year. We know what works because we do it every day for our clients, as well as providing courses and lectures across the country.

Everything I've shared in this book will help you to achieve your goals, provided that you put it into practice daily, as we do.

We worked with a plastic surgeon in Texas who had been running a successful practice for 20 years but had reached an impasse with their marketing strategy. They knew they needed to incorporate social media but hadn't had much success.

We implemented three key marketing strategies without needing to use advertising money or boosting on social media. After building their AMP and setting monthly sales goals, we scheduled their editorial calendar accordingly. We created a monthly cross-promotion and contest for each month. This created the content for weekly marketing e-mails, social posts, written blogs, and video blogs.

Within a matter of months, the numbers began showing consistent growth. At the time of writing they have gained 2,000 new followers, tripling their social media reach! They also increased their revenue by 35 percent.

They achieved these results while cutting other marketing costs, including print and radio. Though they spent less time on marketing than ever before, they started marketing *strategically*.

How does social media increase sales or convert more patients?

Studies show that social media followers purchase from the businesses they follow at a rate of 1 to 5 percent. If 2.5 percent of those 2,000 new followers purchase from the practice within a year's time, that equals 50 patients.

The average patient at the aforementioned practice spends approximately $5,000 a year on services. Based on 50 patients spending $5,000 in a year, the practice can expect to see an increase of approximately $250,000 in sales. It's clear to see that this type of growth has a substantial impact on revenue.

Year	Revenue
2018	
2017	
2016	

Number of Leads per Year	2018	2017	2016	Marketing Spend
Organic SEO Website Inquiries				
Pay Per Click Leads Website				
Social Media				
Real Self				
Physician Locator Website				
Radio				
TV				
Print				
Billboards				
Patient or Staff Referrals				
Physician Referrals				
Paid Social Lead Adv's				
Total				

Practice Statistics	2018	2017	2016
Number of Consultations			
Number of Surgeries perfomed			
Number of Injectable Appointments			
Injectable Cost for the period			
Retail Cost of Goods for the period			
Medical Grade Retail Sales Revenue			
Number of Aesthetic Appointments			

Figure 6: AMP ROI Worksheet

7 IMPLEMENTING AN AMP IN YOUR PRACTICE

7. IMPLEMENTING AN AMP IN YOUR PRACTICE

7.1 NEXT STEPS

Now that we've covered the details of an AMP, I hope it is clear how an AMP will help your practice grow.

When creating your AMP, don't forget the four essentials:

1. Monthly cross-promotions

2. Social media planning

3. E-mail marketing

4. Quarterly sales events

If you implement an AMP with these four essentials, you'll boost your practice's profitability and organization—leading to happy patients and repeat business.

Having a solid AMP in place will increase revenue, reduce impulsive marketing spending, direct patients to new services, maintain your bottom line, even out cash flow, and create high surges of revenue through quarterly sales events.

What's next?

1 HOUR ANNUAL MARKETING PLAN	WHO	DATE	STATUS
1	Who is the lead for your Annual Marketing Plan & implementation?			
2	Who is in charge of emailing clients weekly?			
3	What day and time will your weekly emails go out?			
4	What email management system will you use?			
5	Who is in charge of deciding on the monthly promotions?			
6	Who will design the monthly promotions?			
7	Who and how will you update you patient email list?			
8	Who is responsible to run the social media contest of the month?			
9	Who is responsible for writing blogs?			
10	Who is responsible to video vlogs?			
11	Who will post blogs and vlogs to your website?			
12	Who will post blogs and vlogs to social media platforms?			
13	Who is in charge of deciding on the quarterly events?			
14	Who is in charge of coordinating the event planning?			
15	Who is in charge of keeping your website updated and current?			
16	Who will review website monthly analytic reports?			
17	Who will manage or review SEO results?			
18	Who will manage or review PPC programs?			
19	Who will run quarterly lead reports by lead type?			
20	Who is in charge of quarterly website functionality reviews?			
21	Who is in charge of keeping website content current?			
22	Who will post social media content weekly to FB and IN?			
23	Who is responsible to run social media reports?			
24	Who is responsible to create the editorial calendar and approve?			
25	Who will upload videos to YouTube?			

Figure 7: 1 Hour AMP Action Plan Example

Use the resources provided in this book to build your own AMP and work with your staff to carry out the plan throughout the year. You'll soon be on your way to building a more profitable practice and a more loyal client base.

RESOURCES

Visit

www.projectedgrowthconsulting.com/
ampbook

for downloadable resources.

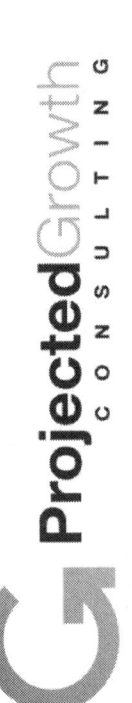

G ProjectedGrowth
C O N S U L T I N G

MARKETING & SOCIAL MEDIA DIAGNOSTIC | YES =1/ NO =0

#	Question	
1	Do you run monthly specials?	
2	Do you utilize cross promotions instead of discounting?	
3	Do you host sales events instead of open houses?	
4	Do you have a client Email List?	
5	Do you update that list monthly?	
6	Do you email your clients weekly with different content and offers?	
7	Do you spend 5% of income on marketing efforts?	
8	Do you track the lead source in your system for all new clients?	
9	Do you know you average cost per lead?	
10	Do you run a report quarterly to look at which lead sources are the best?	
11	Do you look at your marketing budget by line item quarterly?	
12	Do you have an SEO program and or vendor?	
13	Are you consistently doing a PPC campaign?	
14	Do you utilize sales funnel methods to follow and drip on your leads?	
15	Do you automatically send out emails requesting patient reviews?	
16	Is your confirmation process automated by email or texting?	
17	Do you have an automated way to post good reviews on line?	
18	Do you utilize COME back discounts or gift cards?	
19	Do you offer patient financing programs?	
20	Do you have an annual marketing plan by month for the year?	
21	Do you offer a referral rewards to current patients for referring friends?	
22	Do you offer Botox Party programs?	
23	Do you have a client appreciation or VIP event each year?	
24	Do you run a monthly Gift Certificate contest on your website?	
25	Do you run social media contests of the month?	

#	Question	
26	Do you create and post at least 1 blog per month for social and your website?	
27	Do you create and post at least 1 vlog per month for social and your website?	
28	Do you have a Facebook Business Page, and do you know how to access it?	
29	Do you know who has the "Facebook Admin" role for your Page?	
30	Do you post consistently 4-7 times per week on Facebook?	
31	Are your followers growing each month on your social platforms?	
32	Do you have a YouTube Channel?	
33	Do you upload videos monthly to YouTube?	
34	Do you have an Instagram Business Profile, and do you know how to access it?	
35	Do you post consistently 4-7 times per week on Instagram?	
36	Have you looked at your website on a mobile device in the past month?	
37	Do your social media links work on your website?	
38	Do you have a goal for each social media post?	
39	Do you know what Reach is? Or Engagement?	
40	Do you reply to comments and messages on Facebook and Instagram within 24 hours?	
41	Do you have a person in charge of your marketing and social media?	
42	Do you have a person responsible or assigned to follow up on email inquiries?	
43	Do you get back to email inquiries the same day?	
44	Do you get back to online leads within 30 minutes, via email or phone?	
45	Do you track your ROI on marketing? Are you getting a 4X return?	
46	Do you utilize social media reporting systems?	
47	Do you review your website monthly analytic reports?	
48	Do you review your eblasting reports for effectiveness monthly?	
49	Do you respond to on line leads within 15 minutes?	
50	Do you track lead conversion and consultation closing ratios monthly?	
Totals		

BENCHMARKING - How are your doing?	YES =1/ NO =0
WOW - YOU SHOULD TEACH THIS STUFF! CONGRATULATIONS	OVER 25
AVERAGE - WE CAN ROCK THIS PRETTY QUICKLY	11 TO 24
OUCH - WE NEED TO GIVE SOME ATTENTION ASAP	UNDER 10

ANNUAL MARKETING PLAN

	Enter Your Monthly Promo Headline\	Promotion Value Added Cross Promotion
EX:	New Year, New You! .....For example	Free Botox with any Laser Series
JAN		
FEB		
MAR		
APR		
MAY		
JUNE		
JULY		
AUG		
SEPT		
OCT		
NOV		
DEC		

	FaceBook Monthly Contest	Post contest on 1st, award 31st - post winner!
EX:	New Year, New You! .....For example	Pick one of the cross promo items and list below - Botox or Laser
JAN		
FEB		
MAR		
APR		
MAY		
JUNE		
JULY		
AUG		
SEPT		
OCT		
NOV		

Limited To	Retail Value	Image Selection	Design Status	Promo Success
5	$300	SS #1258795	Final Proof	High, Med, Low

Value	Graphic Template	# Entries	Winner	
$ 300.00				

ANNUAL - MONTHLY

MONTH	MONTHLY PROMOTION HEADER/TITLE	PROMOTION | VALUE
Example	New Year, New You!	FREE Botox with Laser Treatment - $250 Value
JAN		
FEB		
MAR		
APR		
MAY		
JUN		
JUL		
AUG		
SEPT		
OCT		
NOV		
DEC		

PROJECTEDGROW

PROMOTIONAL PLANNER

IMAGE #	APPROVED ARTWORK	WEBSITE	SOCIAL MEDIA	E-BLAST	SUCCESS OF PROMO (GREAT, OK, BAD)
Face7	Yes | No	Date	Date	Dates	GREAT

ProjectedGrowth
C O N S U L T I N G

BUILDING YOUR PROMOTION CHECKLIST

1	PROMOTION CREATION	
	What service are you selling?	
	What season or month is the target?	
	Who is the target demo?	
	What would they like for value added?	
	Create the headline	

2	IMAGE SELECTION	
	Select a season appropriate image	
	Select an age appropriate image	
	Select a service appropriate image	
	Is the image attention getting?	
	Is the image what they aspire to be or your demo?	
	Is there direct eye contact?	
	Does this fit your website and marketing theme?	
	Is the image the right layout? Horizontal or vertical	
	Does the image pull you emotionally into it?	

3	BUILDING YOUR PROMOTION	
	Offer of cross promotion is at least 10% value	
	Value is over $100	
	Less than 3 font types	
	3 Selling benefits	
	Fun and catch headline	

	(text cut off)
	Just the details - you want them to call for more info
	White space - make sure you have lot's
	Review on a phone, that where it is usually viewed
	Keep it simple and eye catching
4	**URGENCY AND OFFER**
	While suppplies last or first 5 clients?
	This month only or hard dates?
	Call for details
	Offer not valid with other promotions
	No cash value
	Non transferable
5	**PROOFING**
	Print out the promotion for proofing
	Have multiple people proof
	Check website, phone, address if applicable
	Make sure the link goes to the correct web page
	Set up click here for consultation

ProjectedGrowth
C O N S U L T I N G

PGC Client Lead Source Benchmark Report

Fill in light green shaded squares

Revenue Total		Annual Total
	2018	
	2017	
	2016	

Number of Leads per Year	2018
Organic SEO Website Inquiries	
Pay Per Click Leads Website	
Social Media	
Real Self	
Physician Locator Website	
Radio	
TV	
Print	
Billboards	
Patient or Staff Referrals	
Physician Referrals	
Paid Social Lead Adv's	
Total	

Practice Statistics	2018
Number of Consultations	
Number of Surgeries perfomed	
Number of Injectable Appointments	
Injectable Cost for the period	
Retail Cost of Goods for the period	
Medical Grade Retail Sales Revenue	
Number of Aesthetic Appointments	

	Client Name:	
	Report End Date for YTD:	

Mo Ave	Number of Months

2017	2016	Annual Budget

2017	2016

ProjectedGrowth
C O N S U L T I N G

1-877-742-0742
Info@ProjectedGrowthConsulting.Com
ProjectedGrowthConsulting.Com

1 HOUR ANNUAL MARKETING PLAN		WHO	DATE	STATUS
1	Who is the lead for your Annual Marketing Plan & implementation?			
2	Who is in charge of emailing clients weekly?			
3	What day and time will your weekly emails go out?			
4	What email management system will you use?			
5	Who is in charge of deciding on the monthly promotions?			
6	Who will design the monthly promotions?			
7	Who and how will you update you patient email list?			
8	Who is responsible to run the social media contest of the month?			
9	Who is responsible for writing blogs?			
10	Who is responsible to video vlogs?			
11	Who will post blogs and vlogs to your website?			
12	Who will post blogs and vlogs to social media platforms?			
13	Who is in charge of deciding on the quarterly events?			
14	Who is in charge of coordinating the event planning?			
15	Who is in charge of keeping your website updated and current?			
16	Who will review website monthly analytic reports?			
17	Who will manage or review SEO results?			
18	Who will manage or review PPC programs?			
19	Who will run quarterly lead reports by lead type?			
20	Who is in charge of quarterly website functionality reviews?			
21	Who is in charge of keeping website content current?			
22	Who will post social media content weekly to FB and IN?			

23	Who is responsible to run social media reports?		
24	Who is responsible to create the editorial calendar and approve?		
25	Who will upload videos to YouTube?		
26	Who is responsible to comment and reply to social media?		
27	Who will track incoming leads and consultation closing ratios?		
28	Do you need a social media reporting software?		
29	Who will define and implement a Botox Party Program?		
30	Who is responsible for your referral program and rewards?		
31	Do you want to implement a COME back coupon promotion?		
32	Do you want to have a Gift Certificate Drawing on your website?		
33	Do you need to interview a marketing vendor partner?		
34	Do you need to update or get a new website?		
35	Is your current confirmation system working and who is responsible?		
36	What is your highest reaching post to date?		
37	Do you want to boost posts?		
38	Do you want or have patient financing available?		
39	Do you want to explore sales funnels and lead generation?		
40	Who will segment your email list?		
41	What are the top 3 services you want to grow this year?		
42	Who will track the results of contests and promotions?		
43	Who will coordinate with vendors to get free products?		
44	Who will coordinate with vendors for event support?		
45	Who will analyze overall marketing ROI quarterly?		
46	Who is responsible to make changes to improve marketing?		
47	Who is responsible to decide if you need to outsource social?		
48	Do you need social media content? Where will you get it?		
49	What are the biggest challenges for marketing your practice?		
50	Do you need to add staff or restructure positions for these activities?		

REFERENCES

Aesthetics Surgery Journal, December 2018. Referenced in Plastic Surgery Practice. "Study: Google Placement Favors Physicians' Social Media Presence–Not Smarts and Skills." Last modified December 13, 2018.
http://www.plasticsurgerypractice.com/2018/12/study-google-placement-favors-physicians-social-media-presence-not-smarts-skills/

Bowman, Brian. Consumer Acquisition. "100K Facebook Ads Tested! Here's What Works." Last modified November 9, 2018.
https://www.consumeracquisition.com/100k-facebook-ads-tested-heres-works/

Gallo, Amy. Harvard Business Review. "The Value of Keeping the Right Customers." Last modified October 29, 2014.
https://hbr.org/2014/10/the-value-of-keeping-the-right-customers

Hubspot. "The Ultimate List of Marketing Statistics for 2018." Last modified 2018.
https://www.hubspot.com/marketing-statistics)

Hussain, Anum. Hubspot. "22 Eye-Opening Statistics About Sales Email Subject Lines That Affect Open Rates." Last modified 2019.
https://blog.hubspot.com/sales/subject-line-stats-open-rates-slideshare

Kruse Control Inc. "Rule of 7: How Social Media Crushes Old School Marketing." Last modified March 29, 2018.
https://www.krusecontrolinc.com/rule-of-7-how-social-media-crushes-old-school-marketing/

Leadem, Rose. Entrepreneur. "E-Mail Marketing Field Guide 2018." Last modified May 20, 2017. https://www.entrepreneur.com/article/294536

Moovly. "4 Great Reasons You Should Use Video Marketing." Last modified February 9, 2016. https://www.moovly.com/blog/4-great-reasons-you-should-use-video-marketing

Reichheld, Fred. Bain & Company. "Prescription for Cutting Costs." Last modified October 25, 2001. http://www2.bain.com/Images/BB_Prescription_cutting_costs.pdf

About the author

Kelly Smith is the Founder and CFO of Projected Growth Consulting and an alumna of the University of Washington. Smith has accrued over 20 years' experience as a business consultant, serial entrepreneur, medical spa owner and CFO, and was elected a 2014 VIP of the Year by Worldwide Who's Who. Alongside her semi-virtual team comprising more than 10 women, Smith continues to mentor and grow elective medical practices throughout the US.

A national keynote speaker on business success principles and an editorial contributor and faculty member for multiple industry organizations, Smith presents business and marketing practices on behalf of large laser manufacturers in the cosmetic medical industry. She is a member of Darren Hardy's exclusive High-Performance Alumni Forum and an ambassador for Women's Entrepreneurship Day in Washington and Idaho.

Acknowledgements

My PGC Team:

I cannot thank my team enough for building this successful company and compiling this book with me. My greatest achievement is the company culture and team we now have. This group of women make me happy to go to work and able to face the challenges that have come over the years. I am incredibly blessed to be surrounded by such a capable, driven, and ambitious team. Special thanks to Kim Hadley, Tiffany Vakaloloma, Tanya Weiler, Nina Volostnova, Cindy Constance, Joy DeThorne, Lacey Fuentes, Kelly Sailas, Samantha Johnson, and Stacey Bernhardt. You have all gathered materials, proof-read way too many times and helped to create advice we can be proud to share with our clients and elective medical physicians wishing to grow their practices. Thank you!

I also want to mention and thank Christina Savage and Jacob Longoria for your dedication and expertise for scaling, marketing and strategy!

PGC PROGRAMS

Learn how to grow your practice through on-site events, social media marketing, sales & profit planning, as well as many other options. Through our programs, you will gain access to Strategy Specialists, online materials, cutting edge graphic design, and more!

 OnSite Sales Events

 Social Media Management & Training

 Monthly Business Development & Mastermind Group

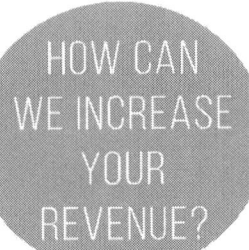 HOW CAN WE INCREASE YOUR REVENUE?

 Annual Marketing Plan, Lead Generation & Sales Funneling

 Online Training Academy

 Benchmarking & Financial Planning

Our team is comprised of industry professionals who understand every challenge that you are facing in your practice, primarily, because we have been where you are now. We have been the owner, the manager, the medical assistant, the consultant and the patient! Eighteen years ago, we found what works – without fail – and we decided we couldn't keep it to ourselves. We want to share it with you and help you run the business of your dreams – and your patient's and staff's dreams!

▶ 877-742-0742
ProjectedGrowthConsulting.Com
Info@ProjectedGrowthConsulting.Com

VIRTUAL TRAINING

ANNUAL MARKETING PLAN COURSE

 Create an Entire Year
Advertising Calendar in Weeks

 Create 12 Monthly
Cross Promotions

 Receive 12 Graphics
for Your Cross Promotions

 Learn to Build Your Social
Media, Blogs, Vlog &
E-Blasting to Support Campaigns

 Create Quarterly
Sales Events

 Utilize Tools to Review ROI
on Current Marketing Efforts

Develop Your Own 12 Month Annual Marketing Plan
Choose a Cross Promo Graphic & Contest Graphic for Each Month!

* You select from our design catalogs, but images are as is without customization.

▶ 877-742-0742

ProjectedGrowth
CONSULTING

ProjectedGrowthConsulting.Com
Info@ProjectedGrowthConsulting.Com

SOCIAL MEDIA
TRAINING
PROGRAM

Our Social Media Training Program is a great solution to create and maintain an online presence in this quickly changing digital World. PGC utilizes proven systems to create proven results!

The 90 Day Comprehensive Social Media Training Program Includes:

- o   Premade Graphic Posting Kit
- o   12 Training Modules
- o   Graphic Design Training for Developing Content
- o   Social Media Editorial Calendars
- o   Contests, Events & E-Blasting Recommendations
- o   Blogging and Vlogging for Search Engine Optimization

Our Social Media Accounts grow 200% on average when these principles are applied. We will show you how to strategically leverage your social media platforms to expand your current business and create new clients. Our proven Contest of the Month process alone can create dramatic increases in reach and growth for your social media presence. Learn how to plan and implement a successful Social Media strategy for your elective medical practice.

▶ 877-742-0742
ProjectedGrowthConsulting.Com
Info@ProjectedGrowthConsulting.Com

GRAPHIC SUBSCRIPTIONS

EXPANDED MARKETING & SOCIAL MEDIA BUNDLES

SUBSCRIPTION BREAKDOWN Promotional Material	STANDARD GRAPHIC BUNDLE	EXPANDED GRAPHIC BUNDLE	PLATINUM GRAPHIC BUNDLE
Monthly Cross Promotional Flyer	✓ (1) Monthly Cross Promo Flyer	✓ (1) Monthly Cross Promo Flyer	✓ (1) Monthly Cross Promo Flyer
Benefit Educational Flyer	✓ (1) Benefit Educational Flyer	✓ (1) Benefit Educational Flyer	✓ (2) Benefit Educational Flyer
Social Media Engagement Posts	✓ (4) Social Media Posts	✓ (8) Social Media Posts	✓ (8) Social Media Posts
Contest of the Month	✓ (1) Contest of the Month	✓ (1) Contest of the Month	✓ (1) Contest of the Month
Written Blogs	✗ No Written Blogs	✓ (2) Written Blogs	✓ (2) Written Blogs
Video Blogs	✗ No Video Blogs	✗ No Video Blogs	✓ (2) Video Blogs
MONTHLY VALUE	$550 VALUE	$1,175 VALUE	$1,675 VALUE
MONTHLY SUBSCRIPTION RATE	$299 / MONTH	$599 / MONTH	$899 / MONTH
MONTHLY SAVINGS	YOU SAVE $251	YOU SAVE $576	YOU SAVE $776
PERCENTAGE SAVINGS	46% SAVINGS	49% SAVINGS	46% SAVINGS

You select from our design catalogs, but images are as is without customization.

ProjectedGrowth
CONSULTING

▶ 877-742-0742
ProjectedGrowthConsulting.Com
Info@ProjectedGrowthConsulting.Com

Made in United States
Orlando, FL
30 January 2023

29239439R00062